NEW YORK CEN
POWER ALONG THE

VOLUME #1 - HARMON

Printed with pride
in the U.S.A.

PHOTOGRAPHS BY EDWARD L. MAY
COMMENTARY BY RICHARD L. STOVING

The Railroad Press
PO Box 444
Hanover, PA 17331-0444

International Standard Book Number 1-931477-16-7

Publishers of:

TRP Magazine

*PRR Lines West
Pittsburgh to St. Louis
1960-1999*

*Illinois Central:
North of the Ohio River*

ALCO's to Allentown

Altoona Action

*Passenger Cars of
New England*

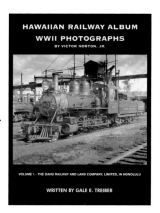

INTRODUCTION

The first I ever knew that there even was an Eddie May was in 1961, when my long-awaited copy of Al Staufer's *Steam Power of the New York Central System, Vol. 1* arrived by mail. Some eight years before, I had first descended the narrow, winding road from Route 9D to the New York Central tracks at Manitou, New York with some high school railfan buddies, and I had been impressed by the manner in which its customary quietude could suddenly be shattered by the passage of a member of the Great Steel Fleet. And here, in Al's book, were photographs of the way Manitou had appeared about a decade before, when steam was king, taken by one Edward L. May. But it would be another five years before I would get to know him.

The occasion was my curiosity, in 1966, to know what a Pacemaker caboose looked like. By that time, Eddie, together with Bill Edson, had published *Locomotives of the New York Central Lines*, and an address for Edson-May Publications in Irvington-on-Hudson was given on the book's title page. So, in an age innocent of the internet and special interest websites, where queries often bring a torrent of information and even pitched battles among the responders, I decided to write to Mr. May to ask if he had any information on the subject.

About two weeks later, an envelope arrived bearing a fine 8x10 photograph of a Pacemaker caboose and a beautifully written response. Eddie was always a good writer. But most amazingly of all, I learned from the return address that he and his wife Claire lived in the same development in Queens, New York, and on the very same street, as did my wife Nancy and I. As he pointed out in his letter, "I would imagine that the part of this letter that catches your eye most is the address." Indeed it did.

We soon became good friends. It's not possible for two people who are so fond of the same things to live in such close proximity and to remain strangers for long. In 1967 Nancy and I moved to a house about two blocks farther away, but our visits to Eddie's apartment became more and more frequent. What a joy it was to be able to talk, talk, and talk about Hudsons, observation cars, Manitou, the *Empire State Express*, water scoops, Grand Central Terminal, locomotive renumberings, Dudley rail, you name it. And, if I happened to ask, because of some current modeling project, "You don't happen to have a right-side view of the 4399 taken between 1945 and 1949, do you?" he'd disappear upstairs (he and Claire had only a two-room duplex; how he squeezed all of his collection into the upstairs bedroom was a miracle) and descend a few minutes later with not one, but *six* photos of the desired subject.

In the late 1970's, Ed had a hankering to visit some of his old haunts, especially on the Catskill Mountain Branch, the old Ulster and Delaware Railroad, and it was my pleasure to accompany him. I remember how delighted he was to discover a faint trace of the "branch of the branch" at Chichester; I remember him pointing out the spot where he, as a child, had gotten his first glimpse of a U&D train west of Kingston; I remember him explaining how both a highway *and* the railroad had managed to squeeze through the Clove; and with sadness I remember his dismay as he viewed what was left of Kingston Point.

In one of my conversations with Eddie in the late 1980's, he mentioned, in a most off-hand way, that he was leaving his entire collection, with the exception of everything associated with the Ulster and Delaware Railroad, to me. I was flabbergasted. I knew that he had many other friends in the railfan community, and I said as much. He replied that most of them were no younger than he, and that he wanted the collection to go to someone younger. I was in my early 50's at the time. I told him that I was honored, and that, if this was his wish, I would always keep the collection intact and attempt to make prints of his negatives or copies of his research documents available to interested railfans to the best of my ability. He seemed content. He said, and I will always remember these words, "Rich, it's my life's work."

In 1991 I retired and, following a dream, moved to rural America, relocating some 260 miles from Queens. Among the few downsides of this move was the fact that I would get to see Eddie less frequently. We corresponded regularly, and in a letter dated January 13, 1993, he asked me to make a trip to his apartment to pick up part of his collection, which I did with great reluctance. Another trip and another load followed in April. Then, in September, Ed's dear wife Claire died, and his health took a turn for the worse. Although we continued to chat on the telephone, his last letter to me was dated November 10, 1993.

In 1995, Ed's nephew arranged for him to enter a retirement home near Dallas, Texas. He then asked me to come to Ed's vacated apartment once more to pick up anything remaining that related to New York Central, and I visited the place where I had enjoyed so many happy conversations for the last time. With a heavy heart, I brought the last remnants of Ed's collection home. Telephone conversations continued, and I sincerely wish that I had been forthright in asking him some more pointed questions about parts of his collection, especially concerning the meaning of some of the coding in his negative index books. But it's hard to ask such questions, because it's hard to accept the fact that there may come a time when they cannot be answered. The time came on December 22, 1998, when Ed died from cardiac arrest in Dallas at the age of 80.

I'd been printing black-and-white 35mm and 2-inch by 2-inch negatives for years on a little Omega B-22 enlarger, and I had arranged to have a proper darkroom built in my new home, but Eddie's negatives were mostly in the 2-1/2-inch by 4-1/4-inch format, and this far exceeded the capacity of the B-22. Aching to produce some really nice prints of Eddie's work, I purchased in 2000 a Model 45 Beseler enlarger capable of handling much larger negatives, a box of 8x10 paper, and dug in. What a thrill it was to see new images appearing on paper in the developing tray.

Eddie's primary photographic interest was in locomotives. He was one of the "engine picture kids," young men with cameras who frequented engine terminals in the pre-war years to get and to trade rods-down shots of as many locomotives as possible, and because of this interest there are vastly more still shots in his collection than action photos. Although Ed photographed locomotives of many railroads, he was surely most interested in New York Central power, and that interest led him very often to Harmon. As nearly as I have been able to determine, Ed visited Harmon 28 times between 1935 and 1951, twelve before he went into the service of his country during World War II, and sixteen after he returned to civilian life.

Eddie apparently had the reasonable trust of at least some of the railroad workers at Harmon, because it's clear that he was able to wander around the facilities there without incurring too much displeasure. It would be impossible today to take the kinds of photographs that Eddie took more than a half-century ago without all manner of red tape and without constant official supervision. The fact that he was able to obtain, from certain employees, documents such as locomotive mileage and inspection reports, out-of-date classification books, employee timetables, and the original historical record cards for engines as they were whitelined, testifies to his general acceptance around Harmon's hallowed halls.

In the preparation of this book, I had to reach a decision regarding the use of previously published photographs. Ed combed his collection for what he considered to be his best efforts for inclusion in several books that have been printed over the years, most especially Al Staufer's *Steam Power of the New York Central System Vol. 1*, *Later Power*, and *Thoroughbreds*. The question arose, should some of these photographs be reprinted here? I answered the question in the affirmative, because it seemed right to me that a book of Ed May's photographs ought to include some of his best work. I believe there are ten photos in this book that were published in the Staufer books.

Like most of the "engine picture kids," Eddie traded photos with other rail photographers, and quite a few of the negatives in his collection are the work of others. In seeking to include some interesting or representative material in this book that Ed either chose not to photograph (such as a Budd RDC-1) or missed photographing (such as Niagara 6000 before the application of smoke deflectors), I have used seventeen images not photographed by Eddie, but nevertheless printed from original negatives in his collection. Wherever possible, I have credited the original photographers in the commentaries.

With the exception of the photograph of the restored builder's plate from Hudson 5201, all of the photos that appear in this book were personally printed by me. In most cases it took many attempts to get the best print possible from a negative. Some of the early negatives are too thin or too dense. I owe much to the memory of another dear departed friend, Hubert (Stocky) Stockwell, who taught me many darkroom tricks. Finding appropriate negatives, printing them, writing the commentary, and working to put this book together have all been parts of a labor of love.

Many readers will notice that, in referring to steam locomotives, I have used the feminine pronouns "she" and "her," while diesel and electric locomotives are simply "its." I have done this not to anger any dyed-in-the-wool diesel or electric railfans, but rather to honor the convention that Eddie usually employed. Eddie, like most of us who remember them, regarded steam locomotives as almost living creatures that, like ships of the sea, always merit personification. Regarding electrics, however, I could not bring myself to be so consistent in style as to refer to the dowager S-1 100 as an "it." One hundred years old as of this writing, she deserves to be a "she."

In a sense, this is Ed May's book, and in writing the commentaries I have tried to put as much of him into it as I could. High green Eddie, wherever you are!

Richard L. Stoving
November, 2004

ACKNOWLEDGEMENTS

To the best of my knowledge, there are seventeen photographs in this book that were not taken by Ed May, but that were printed from original negatives in his collection. It is possible that there are even more. In my commentaries, I have credited each additional photographer wherever Ed May's indices provided a name, and I am grateful to all, known or unknown.

I am also very grateful to Harold Crouch, John Ham, Fred Furminger, Maurice Lewman, and Charles M. Smith, and to the various authors whose works are listed in my bibliography.

I further wish to thank Larry Auerbach, Maxine Jacobson, and Elaine Massena for the assistance they provided at the Westchester County Historical Society and the Westchester County Archives and Record Center.

Thanks are also extended to Jaime F. M. Serensits at The Railroad Press for his support for this project and for his professional guidance.

Most of all, I thank my wife Nancy for her untiring readings and rereadings of the various drafts of the text, and for her careful reading of the final proofs.

Harmon owes its name to real estate developer Clifford B. Harmon, who in 1907 purchased part of the Van Cortlandt property along the Croton River to develop the area as a community for artists, writers, and musicians. The Wagnerian soprano Lillian Nordica helped him to publicize his development; Nordica Hill is named for her. On his property he built a Japanese-style "Nikko Inn," which became a favorite retreat for such early film stars as Mary Pickford and Douglas Fairbanks.

When Harmon learned that the New York Central and Hudson River Railroad wished to establish a permanent location for the exchange of electric and steam motive power, he agreed to sell a section of his land to the railroad on the condition that the station there would always be named after him, and that it would become a stop for all trains. Since there was no possibility of changing locomotives without stopping, it may be assumed that the railroad agreed without much hesitancy.

OPPOSITE: With the T motor in the clear, the air test complete, and a highball from the conductor, J3a 5437 blasts out of Harmon with the second section of #67, the *Commodore Vanderbilt*, on a chilly March 23, 1941 afternoon. Unless you wanted a speed shot, Harmon was the place to go to photograph New York Central power, be it steam, diesel, or electric.

ABOVE: If ever there was a ubiquitous steam locomotive type, it was the USRA-designed 0-8-0 switcher. A total of 1,375 of them were built, and they went to many railroads. On the New York Central, they were classed as U3 locomotives, and there were 446 of them on its roster by 1946, more than any other NYC locomotive class. The 7711 was built by Lima in August, 1922 and is seen here at Harmon on May 21, 1950.

OPPOSITE ABOVE: The Central maintained a total of 376 0-6-0 switchers in 1944, 155 of them in class B10. The B10's were built continuously from 1903 through 1912. Sunning herself in Harmon on May 26, 1946 is B10v 6701, a 1912 product of Alco's Pittsburgh works. A missing dome casing provides a partial view of the engine's safety valves.

OPPOSITE BELOW: In 1944 Central also rostered a fleet of 121 B11 0-6-0 switchers. Can you spot any significant differences? I don't believe there are any. Why the new class designation? The easiest explanation seems to be that, in subclassing the B10's, Central simply ran out of letters sometime around 1912. That's right, there were 26 subclasses of B10's, running all the way from B10a to B10z. What to do? Start in again with B11a. There are other possible explanations involving superheating and the temporary classification of some earlier 0-6-0's as B11's, but the one given above is probably the best. The 6722, a member of subclass B11k, came from Alco-Schenectady in 1913 and was retired in 1950. The date here is February 8, 1941.

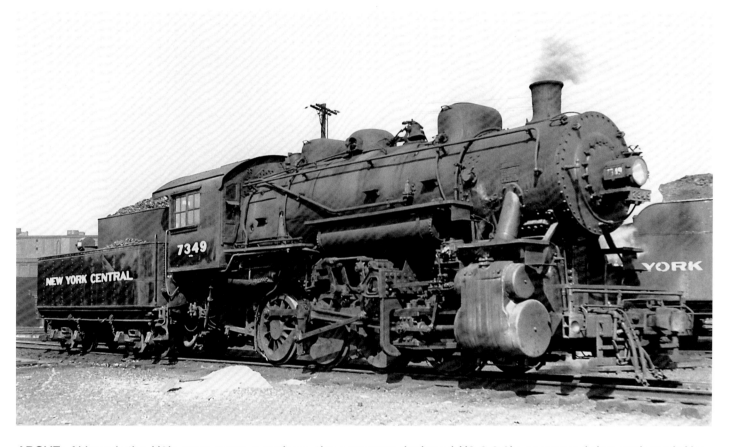

ABOVE: Although the U3's were more populous, the company-designed U2 0-8-0's possessed that trademark New York Central "look." The U2's had 58" diameter drivers, six inches greater than the U3's, and were more typically found in passenger switching service than in freight. The 7349 is a member of subclass U2d, and was built at Alco's Pittsburgh works in August, 1917. She is seen here at Harmon on April 13, 1947.

In 1908 Harmon published a brochure outlining the virtues of Harmon Park, a housing development to be situated east of the Harmon rail facility. "Being the terminus of the electric zone, every train, even the Empire State Express and the Twentieth Century Limited will stop at Harmon to exchange motive power," his brochure explained. "Thus," it continued, "Harmon Park can boast a train service equaled by no other suburb in the vicinity of New York." The brochure also promised prospective buyers that the railroad's terminal buildings, shops, and yards would be in a deep cut, completely hidden from view. Nothing was said about the smoke that would rise from the location for years to come.

Harmon, the man, went on to earn a favorable reputation as a World War I pilot and aviation pioneer, while Harmon, the engine terminal, developed a reputation of its own, tolerable among passengers when engine changes were effected quickly, less so when there were delays. The electrification project was completed by 1913, with facilities at Harmon including a 25-stall roundhouse and an 85-foot turntable. A second, 31-stall roundhouse with a 100-foot turntable was added in 1928. Coaling was by trestle, with a storage capacity of 900 tons. Company records show that daily coal usage in 1941 was 830 tons in the summer and 935 tons in the winter. Although unsubstantiated, it has been said that 1,200 tons of coal were once dumped on a single day, probably during World War II. In 1941, 357 persons were employed by the railroad at Harmon in the summer and 323 in the winter. Assigned work included both light and heavy running repairs.

On August 7, 1953 Niagara 6020 was the last steam engine to be dispatched west from Harmon, with twenty-odd employees waving a final farewell. The 1928 round-house was razed shortly thereafter, but a portion of the 1913 house remained standing into the 1960's. Harmon continues to be an important repair and maintenance facility for the Metro-North Railroad.

BELOW: The earliest of Ed's visits to Harmon appears to have been on April 27, 1935, a little over a month after his seventeenth birthday. His negative collection contains eleven shots taken by him on that day, including this view of C class 1003, one of the only two photographs he ever took of a Central 4-4-0. Like many of us, Ed often said that he wished he'd been born a little earlier to see those things on the railroad that he missed. For him it was the famous Buchanan 4-4-0's and the K2 Pacifics. For a later generation it would be any New York Central steam at all, and for an even later generation, the New York Central System itself. The 1003 was originally NYC&HR 877, built at Schenectady in October, 1890. Ed caught her just in time; she was scrapped in the following year. Even here, she's in trouble; look closely and you'll see that her main drivers and rods have been removed.

OPPOSITE ABOVE: Another senior citizen living on borrowed time at Harmon was this class E Mogul. With a cover on her stack, she was in storage at Harmon on February 22, 1946. Ed said the 1905 had been used to help with the removal of the tracks of the Getty Square branch of the Putnam Division, being the only available steam locomotive light enough to be permitted on the branch. 2-6-0's were prime freight movers on the Central in the 1890's and the early years of the Twentieth Century, and a significant number of the larger E1 class survived into the 1940's to perform duties where weight restrictions presented problems. The 1905 was built at Schenectady in June, 1892 as NYC&HR 722, and survived until December, 1947.

OPPOSITE BELOW: Not quite as venerable but only four months away from the end of a long and useful career, here is F12a 1236. She had been built by Alco-Schenectady in 1906 as a member of class F2a, but when superheated she and most of her sisters in all of the F2 subclasses were reclassified as F12 engines. The F2's were originally built to handle fast freight movements but were soon replaced in that service by the K11 Pacifics. Nevertheless, 58 of the original 137 NYC F12's were still in service on New York Central by 1946, finding a variety of useful chores including service on the railroad's Putnam Division. Although the 1236's main rods and much of her valve gear have been removed, it can be seen that Baker gear was applied to this locomotive in place of her original Stephenson linkage. The date is October 31, 1948.

OPPOSITE ABOVE: Orphaned off the Boston and Albany by that company's dieselization program, H5g 1216 was caught lounging at Harmon on April 23, 1949 by Ed's friend and fellow-railfan William Curtis. Although there were more H5's on New York Central and its subsidiary lines than any other class of road engine, they were rarely seen on the Hudson Division by the 1940's. This engine started life in 1905 as a G5g 2-8-0, B&A 2592, was renumbered 992 in 1912, and was converted in August of 1915 to a 2-8-2 locomotive as part of a massive program that involved the rebuilding of 462 class G5 locomotives. In 1951 she was renumbered NYC 1351, only to be retired in the following year.

OPPOSITE BELOW: Perhaps the most unsung heroes of the New York Central motive power fleet were the K3 Pacifics. Two hundred and eighty-one K3's were built continuously from 1911 through 1925, and they were the standard for mainline passenger service until the advent of the Hudsons. These were the engines depicted hauling the *20th Century Limited* on the famous Central calendar portraits from 1923 to 1927. One hundred and sixty-six were still rostered by the Central after World War II. On one of his early visits to Harmon, Ed appears to have caught the attention of the engineman and fireman of K3a 3434. The date is April 4, 1936, and this engine will be renumbered 4810 before the end of the year. None of the engines in the primordial subclass K3a lasted past 1939.

ABOVE: "C" stood for Baldwin when it came to New York Central K3 and K11 Pacifics. The only K3's that Baldwin built for the Central were in subclass K3c, and similarly the only Baldwin K11's were in subclass K11c. Just as New York Central's arch rival Pennsylvania Railroad rarely purchased steam locomotives from Alco, Central rarely contracted with Baldwin for steam power. Doubtlessly this had something to do with location; Baldwin was down in Pennsy territory while Alco-Schenectady was on line, of course, in Schenectady. Curiously, one of the Baldwin K3's of 1912, 4825, seen here in May of 1946, outlived all of the earlier K3a and K3b engines, as well as many engines in the later subclasses, by surviving until May of 1950. Perhaps this was just a quirk of fate, but it could suggest that Baldwin built a pretty good machine. Baldwin's round builder's plate can be seen high on 4825's smokebox, partially hidden by the handrail.

TOP: Among the numerous members of the K3n subclass was the 4724, seen here on May 11, 1946, probably ready to head a local west to Poughkeepsie. While many K3's were ultimately equipped with booster engines and stokers, this engine was not one of them, as evidenced by the fact that she still has her original Cole trailing truck. It looks as if the hogger is enjoying a sandwich for lunch.

ABOVE: Equipped with footboards to facilitate her end-of-career use in local freight service, sister K3n 4730 looks a lot less racy and has a decidedly stubby, hang-dog look. It's April 25, 1948, and this once-proud locomotive will be retired in January of the following year.

BELOW: The final development of Central's very successful K3 fleet was the appearance, in 1925, of five K3r locomotives built by Alco-Brooks for the Big Four and numbered originally 6500-6504. With a number of specifications and dimensions quite unlike all other K3's, these engines might well have been classified differently, but this was not the case. They could move; a reliable source once told me that the 4803 was at times run at speeds up to 115 miles per hour between Anderson, Indiana and Louisville, Kentucky on the Big Four. In the system-wide renumbering of 1936 they became NYC 4800-4804. The 4804 is seen here at Harmon in July of 1951. The K3r engines were the first to be built for the system with pilot-mounted air compressors, a feature that would become standard on later power. The 4804 was retired in October, 1952 and sold for scrap in February of the following year.

BOTTOM: Looking a bit worn and weary at Harmon on April 6, 1946, is K11d 4522. Originally built between 1910 and 1913 for fast freight service, the K11's resembled their K3 cousins, but were equipped with 69-inch, rather than 79-inch, drivers. Two hundred of them were built, the first 50 originally in subclass K10a before superheating. Replaced as primary freight power by the arrival of the L1 Mohawks in 1916, 102 of them continued in service into the 1940's, and an additional 28 were converted to K14 engines with 72-inch drivers. This is an unattributed photo from Ed May's collection.

BELOW: Among the K14's rebuilt from K11's was this K14g, one of fifteen that were converted for the Boston and Albany Railroad, where they served as the passenger power of choice until the arrival of the K6 Pacifics in 1925. This engine, seen at Harmon on July 7, 1951, had been B&A 580, but has recently been renumbered as NYC 4380.

BOTTOM: Looking very much as built, J1b Hudson 5201, the first production Hudson built after the experimental J1a 5200, stands ready for service in Harmon on December 5, 1937. Few could argue with the aesthetics of these early Hudsons before time and modifications took their toll on appearance.

OPPOSITE BELOW: Cast iron builder's plates were difficult to remove, so many of them went to scrap with their locomotives. This one, from the 5201, was saved and has been beautifully restored. NYC records say that 5201 rolled out of Alco-Schenectady in September 1927, although this plate carries an August 1927 date.

TOP: We can be sure that the photo of the 5201 on the opposite page shows her ready to take a train west, because this photo, taken by Eddie a short time later on the same day, shows her doing just that. She is leaving Harmon with #5, the *Mohawk*.

ABOVE: Here, in a photo taken by Bill Curtis, is the same 5201 again, now nearing the end of her career on July 7, 1952. She was retired in July of the following year. I have a copy of a letter from A. L. Prentice, a New York Central vice president, dated November 9, 1955. It states that this locomotive, along with thirteen others, was to be sold to Luria Brothers & Co. for scrap at $43.75 per gross ton. Tonnage of the 5201 with tender is shown to be 460,200 pounds, so her owners got $10,066 and change for her. For that amount, it's too bad somebody couldn't have saved her.

OPPOSITE ABOVE: Clear air and a low sun at the right angle helped Ed to capture twenty-nine of his very best loco-motive portraits on a very successful visit to Harmon on December 5, 1937. Here J1b 5205 stands on the ready track awaiting a call to duty. Ed considered the early J1's, as built and as seen here, with straight running boards, Walschaerts valve gear, and Roman lettering, to be the best looking of all New York Central steam power.

OPPOSITE BELOW: Truly an Ed May classic is this view of an engineer "oiling around" on J1c 5272, with sister 5250 right next door. I can almost smell the valve oil. It's April 4, 1936.

BELOW: Here's the same 5272 departing Harmon about two years later, on June 18, 1938, with train #53, a late after-noon Albany local. There's no air conditioning in the coaches for comfort, and there are no chains across those open baggage car doors for safety!

BOTTOM: The J1d's get my vote for the most handsome of all Hudsons, probably because I like the sunken Elesco feedwater heaters. I find the Baker valve gear intriguing as well. Here's the last NYC J1d, 5314, at Harmon in an early Ed May shot dated April 4, 1936. Obviously, Ed had a pretty decent camera when he was a teenager.

ABOVE: Here comes J1d 5305, slipping into Harmon on October 22, 1939 with train #40, the *North Shore Limited*. It looks as if another rail photographer further out on the platform has already taken his picture and is now watching the arrival. After the Hudson is cut off, a T-motor will speed this train down to Grand Central Terminal. Stand back, please!

OPPOSITE: Another Ed May classic shows J1d 5311 coming through the wash rack at Harmon on October 27, 1939. Keeping a fleet of steam locomotives looking clean was no easy task, but, at least with primary passenger power, Central did try.

OPPOSITE ABOVE: J1e was the final J1 subclass, comprised of 40 locomotives, 30 for New York Central, numbers 5315-5344; and ten for the CCC&St.L, originally 6620-6629 in the Big Four numbering scheme, but renumbered 5395-5404 under the system-wide renumbering of 1936. The last NYC J1e, 5344, was streamlined as the *Commodore Vanderbilt* in 1934 and completely rebuilt with the Dreyfuss-style streamlining in 1939. Here at Harmon on April 13, 1947 is a less-celebrated member of the J1e clan, but one that is probably every bit as capable as her famous sister. The wisp of steam escaping from her auxiliary stack is probably exhaust from her air compressors.

OPPOSITE BELOW: There is an element of sadness inherent in this photograph. It depicts 5315, the first NYC J1e, approaching Harmon from the west with train #54, the *Mohawk*, on October 22, 1939, and it is the only photograph Ed ever took of this engine. In April of the following year, she would be destroyed in the disastrous wreck of train #19, the *Lake Shore Limited*, at Little Falls, New York. The 5315 was the only New York Central Hudson that would not complete a full service life.

ABOVE: Orphaned off the Boston and Albany by Rudolf Diesel's invention, the B&A 75"-drivered Hudsons found several more years of useful existence on the River and Harlem Divisions. Originally numbered B&A 600-619, all were renumbered NYC 5455-5474 in April, 1951. B&A J2b 605 sits ready for work here at Harmon on May 21, 1950, before renumbering.

TOP: Outshopped at Schenectady in the previous month, J3a 5442 posed at Harmon for this beautiful portrait on December 5, 1937. Ed said she was ready to head out on her first revenue assignment.

OPPOSITE: On the same day, Ed photographed the front end of sister 5441, presumably also ready for her first assignment. You can be sure that Ed knew that nobody was in 5441's cab when he stood in the gauge to take this shot. The J3 engines were the first to be built with the New York Central oval displayed under the road number on the headlight shelf. This was a nice touch, and it would be repeated on converted L2 Mohawks 2995 and 2998 as well as on all future L3 and L4 engines.

ABOVE: Twelve years and a world war later, the J3's presented a very different appearance. Here's the first J3a, 5405 on June 5, 1949. It would be difficult to enumerate the changes that have been made, but the huge PT tender would top the list. That tender, when loaded, weighed 30 tons more than the engine!

NYC Power Along the Hudson

BELOW: New York Central's prewar, all-new *20th Century Limited* was inaugurated on June 15, 1938, which was a Wednesday. By 1938 Ed was presumably gainfully employed, but he managed to get to Harmon three days later on Saturday to see what all the fuss was about. He took a number of photographs of at least two of the ten J3a Hudsons that were especially streamlined to handle the new train. These two of the 5451 are among the best.

TOP: Ed moved over to his favorite spot for photographing westbound departures by the time the 5451 steamed out of Harmon with #25, the *Century*. If the train is on time (and it had better be!) it's 5:46 by the conductor's standard time watch; 6:46 by Ed's daylight savings time watch. This is probably the 5451's first trip westward.

ABOVE: In 1941 New York Central ordered 32 stainless steel passenger equipment cars from Budd for use on an all-new *Empire State Express*, the company's venerable deluxe coach train that was carded to cross the Empire State, New York to Buffalo, in a little less than eight hours. For the head end, Central selected two standard J3a engines, 5426 and 5429, and decorated them with black lacquer and some tastefully applied stainless steel shrouding. The result was indeed eye-catching, but, as is well known, no worse day could have been chosen for the inaugural run – December 7, 1941. Needless to say, the train's first trips received little or no notice in the media. Streamlining was not removed from the 5429 until June of 1949, and from the 5426 until November of 1950, by which time both engines had been equipped with PT tenders. Bill Curtis caught the 5429 on film at Harmon on June 16, 1946. She still possesses some of her 1941 elegance in spite of the loss of some skirting and her missing front coupler cover.

TOP: In the pre-war period, no engines could be said to be more representative of freight power on the Hudson Division than the L2a Mohawks. With their forward-hung Elesco feedwater heaters, pilot-mounted air compressors, and squared-off superheater headers, every inch of them bespoke the power necessary to muscle 100-car manifest freights up the Hudson. The 2777 is seen here at Harmon on February 23, 1946, having encountered a small snow bank in the performance of her most recent task.

ABOVE: Following close on the heels of the L2a's of 1926, the L2c's arrived in 1929. The most obvious difference was a cleaned-up appearance, consistent with management's thinking toward the end of the decade. This prewar shot of L2c 2878 was taken on Ed's very successful visit to Harmon on December 5, 1937.

BELOW: The final L2 Mohawks were 75 L2d locomotives from Alco-Schenectady, 25 for the Big Four as 6225-6249, and 50 for NYC as 2450-2499. They were all renumbered to NYC 2925-2999 in 1936. Here's the highest-numbered L2d at Harmon in a photo taken in 1947 by Bill Curtis. Sister L2d's 2995 and 2998 were chosen in 1939 to be converted to dual-service locomotives, obtaining lightweight revolving and reciprocating parts, improved cross-balancing, roller bearings, and a number of other modifications. They performed well in passenger service and were the precursors of the 25 dual-service L3a engines that would be ordered in the following year.

BOTTOM: Less than two months old here on February 8, 1941, L3a 3024 will play a major role in moving the men and materials necessary to win a war that America will join in ten months. After the war, her good looks and those of her L3 and L4 sisters will be greatly diminished by the application of smoke deflectors. This is an unattributed photo from Eddie's collection, but it may have been taken by Ed's long-time friend, F. Ray McKnight. A lot of negative swapping went on among the "engine picture kids."

OPPOSITE: I'd love to be able to say with certainty that the young man posing on the pilot of the 3024 at Harmon on the same February 1941 day is Eddie May, but, unfortunately, I can't be sure. If it is, he's 22 years old. I knew him when he was in his fifties, sixties, and seventies, and I can't say that there's much resemblance, but then I don't look much like I did when I was in my twenties, either. I can tell you that he made a big thing about always wearing a hat, that the picture was probably taken, like the one above of the same engine, by his buddy Ray McKnight, and that if Ed could have mugged for a camera on the pilot of a brand new locomotive at Harmon, he probably would have. At the very least, it's a great front-end shot of this brand new L3a.

BELOW: In addition to the 25 dual-service L3a Mohawks, an equal number of engines in subclass L3b were ordered. Perhaps because of the looming threat of war, these engines were intended principally for freight service. Ten L3b's, numbered 3025-3034, came from Alco-Schenectady, and fifteen, 3035-3049, came from Lima, all between November 1940 and January 1941. The Lima engines were equipped with semi-sunken Elesco feedwater heaters, providing a unique front-end appearance, while the Alco engines came with Worthington heaters. Booster engines and footboards proclaimed their intended use, although all could provide steam heat and a few came equipped with air signal apparatus for emergency passenger service. Having moved an immeasurable amount of war-winning tonnage in her first five years, here is Lima's 3037 at Harmon on February 23, 1946.

BELOW: The L3a Mohawks were delivered with 69-inch drivers, the standard for fast freight engines on New York Central all the way back to the F2 ten-wheelers of 1905. However, one L3a, the 3000, was soon refitted with 72-inch drivers. As such, her performance in dual service must have been impressive, because when wartime traffic demanded that Central continue to augment its dual-service fleet, 50 72-inch-drivered L4 locomotives were the result. These were real war babies, with engines in subclass L4a arriving between December 1942 and March 1943, and engines in subclass L4b appearing between October 1943 and January 1944. All 50 engines came from Lima. Her war-winning years behind her, L4a Mohawk 3114 relaxes at Harmon on April 13, 1947. Starting with the L1 engines of 1916, Central eschewed the industry-wide convention of calling 4-8-2 locomotives "Mountains." On a railroad that touted its water-level route between New York City and Buffalo, such a name would have been unthinkable. So all 600 of the 4-8-2's built for the New York Central and its subsidiaries were called Mohawks.

OPPOSITE ABOVE: Eddie photographed one of the ultimate Mohawks, L4b 3138, during one of his postwar visits to Harmon on July 24, 1949. Aside from the road numbers, one easy way to identify an L4b was by its multiple bearing crossheads. Another give-away was the dome behind the tender's coal bunker. It was part of an overflow control system that allowed engines so equipped to take water from track pans at speeds up to 80 miles per hour. To the best of my knowledge, no L3 or L4a engines were so equipped.

OPPOSITE BELOW: Steam's finest attainments on the Central could be credited to the modest fleet of 25 4-8-4 S1b Niagaras, locomotives that challenged the incoming diesels in every performance arena and beat them in many. Rolling up incredible mileage records, they seemed to be everywhere at once, but their lives were short. Most of them were scrapped before their tenth birthday. The 6021, seen here on February 22, 1946, was built at Schenectady in January of the same year, and was sold for scrap in September of 1955.

OPPOSITE ABOVE: Two of the Niagaras were not S1b's. The first Niagara, NYC 6000, was the only member of class S1a. Owing to a wartime restriction, she was originally fitted with 75" drivers, and, unlike the S1b's, she did not roll out of Schenectady equipped with smoke deflectors. She is seen here as-built at Harmon on August 26, 1945, just five months after her construction and just twelve days after VJ Day. She will very soon trade her 75" drivers for 79" wheels, the standard for NYC passenger power for nearly half a century. I've commented that smoke deflectors applied to the L3 and L4 Mohawks detracted from their good looks, but, in looking at this photo, I think I'm glad that this engine soon got them, and that the other Niagaras got them from the start. This and the photograph below it were taken by Bill Curtis.

OPPOSITE BELOW: The other "different" Niagara was NYC 5500, the sole member of class S2a, seen here at Harmon on June 18, 1950. The 5500 differed principally from her S1b sisters in the design of her tender and in that she was equipped with poppet valves rather than conventional piston valves. Exhaustive tests were performed to determine whether poppet valve steam admission could be seen as superior, but the issue soon became moot owing to management's overwhelming endorsement of internal combustion motive power.

ABOVE: Would you believe a diesel-electric locomotive riding on archbar trucks? Believe! This little creature, a one-of-a-kind on the Central, was originally built in 1923 by General Electric as a battery-powered switcher for Bethlehem Steel Company. A 250-horsepower Buda 4-cylinder engine was added about 1930, and New York Central purchased the locomotive for switching in lower Manhattan in June of 1933. Originally NYC 1505, it was renumbered 505 in 1936 and is seen here at Harmon on December 5, 1937. It was sold to Eastman Kodak in 1944. Few people had any difficulty determining which end was which on most steam engines, but when it came to diesels, especially one that looked like this, there could be problems, and whether a movement was to be considered as forward or as backward depended on which end was the front of the locomotive. So markings had to be applied, not only to diesels, but also to electric locomotives and MU equipment. The "B" on the side of this locomotive designated that it was the left, or fireman's side. The engineer's controls were on the "A" side. Forward of the engineer's normal position was the front, or number "1" end, also marked with an "F." The number 2 end, closest to Eddie in this photograph, was considered to be the rear of the locomotive.

OPPOSITE ABOVE: Not one to pass up photographing something unusual, Ed caught another one-of-a-kind, DE-F 510, basking in the sun outside of the electric shop at Harmon on October 20, 1939. Three firms conspired in 1928 to produce this experimental freight locomotive: Alco, GE, and Ingersol-Rand. Originally NYC 1550, it was renumbered 1510 in 1929, 510 in 1936, and 500 in 1941. It was ultimately rebuilt into a diesel hump trailer but scrapped in 1953.

OPPOSITE BELOW: One of Boston and Albany's Alco "high hood" units, DES-7b 684, caught Ed's fancy as it switched freight cars at Harmon on April 25, 1948. Later in the year it will be renumbered 810. This unit is one of eleven acquired from Alco-G.E. in 1939 and retired in 1962-1963.

ABOVE: Center-cab switchers certainly provided good visibility for the engineer in both directions, but again the front-versus-rear designations were critical. General Electric built eight of these little 330 horsepower, 70-ton switchers for New York Central, NYC 506-513, between 1940 and 1942. The 511 is seen at Harmon on April 18, 1948; the 507 is showing some of its innards on March 26, 1950.

BELOW: DCA-2a 3201 was not a one-of-a-kind, but close to it. On Central there were only four of these units, 3200-3203. Built by Baldwin in 1947 and 1948, they were extremely unpopular with crews owing to a bouncy ride that was finally corrected only by the substitution of Alco trucks with a longer wheelbase. Nicknamed "Gravel Gerties" after the less-than-glamorous character in the Dick Tracy comic strips, Central retired these units in 1960 and scrapped them in 1962. Eddie encountered the 3201 on May 21, 1950, after it had acquired its Alco drop-equalized trucks.

BOTTOM: By 1951, what Eddie ruefully called the "stinkwagons" had so invaded Harmon that he rarely visited his old haunt. But his friend Bill Curtis continued to visit, and this image, now in Eddie's collection, of DFA-6a 5012 and an unidentified companion "A" unit, both 1950 Fairbanks Morse products, were lensed by him. The date is August 5, 1951. There were twelve of these "A" units, NYC 5006-5017. All were rebuilt with EMD 567 engines at Collinwood in 1955 and 1956, and all were retired by 1965.

TOP: In 1946, few could imagine that steam would be gone from Harmon forever within eight years. After all, the L4 Mohawks were only 3-year-old war babies, and brand new Niagaras were still appearing on the property. Given that the life expectancy of a steam locomotive was perhaps 30 years (the Mogul that we saw on page 9 dated back at least 50 years, didn't she?) these giants would surely be around until 1970, right? Wrong! But nobody knew how quickly the show would be over. So it was probably with some degree of condescension that Ed allowed himself to photograph, on Washington's Birthday, 1946, DPA-1a 4005. It was different. It was a novelty. Why not?

ABOVE: A year and a month later, an A-B-A set of brand-new Alco freight units ground their way westbound through Harmon. There was no law prohibiting diesels from operating on the Island of Manhattan, so they probably brought this train up the West Side freight line all the way from the West 72nd Street freight yards. The date is March 29, 1947.

TOP: The final and perhaps most handsome of all New York Central's EMD "covered wagons" were 60 DPA-5 units, more popularly known as E-8's. They were numbered 4036-4095, and delivered between 1951 and 1953. Bill Curtis caught the first of the clan, 4036, and a companion "A" unit at Harmon on September 8, 1951.

ABOVE: Thought by many to be the most beautiful diesel-electric locomotives ever built, Alco's PA-1's and PA-2's surely looked grand in the light-on-dark gray lightning stripe scheme that resulted from livery conceived by Henry Dreyfuss for the 1948 *20th Century Limited*. By July 21, 1951, when Ed took this picture of DPA-4a 4208, the novelty of diesel propulsion had long expired, and it was painfully clear that Eddie's "stinkwagons" would soon vanquish steam power forever.

BELOW: What is it? It's New York Central's very first 3-power locomotive. It could run on third-rail power, on power supplied by its 240-cell storage battery and its 300-horsepower diesel engine combined, or on its storage battery alone. The battery could be charged from the third rail or by the engine. Classed as DES-2, and originally numbered 1525, it was produced through the combined efforts of Alco, General Electric, and Ingersol-Rand. It was the only member of its class, but it was the precursor of the DES-3 3-power units that followed in 1930. The 1525 was renumbered 525 in 1936 and is pictured here at Harmon on October 1, 1939.

BOTTOM: The production model 3-power locomotives had a more conventional appearance. Forty-one DES-3 units were built as NYC 1526-1562 and MCRR 7530-7533. Their unique design permitted the 3-power units to stray from third-rail power for a couple of hours if necessary, at times a very useful convenience. Engine 554, originally 1554, is seen here on May 21, 1950.

BELOW: Seven class Q motors were built in 1926 by Alco and General Electric to handle switching chores on its Electric Division, including the rebuilt West Side freight line. Originally numbered 1250-1256, they were renumbered 150-156 in 1936. Ed found the 155 at rest at Harmon on May 21, 1950.

BOTTOM: Take four Q-motor trucks and put them under a pair of semi-permanently coupled car bodies and you're on the way toward creating the two units of a class R-A electric locomotive. But don't be too disappointed if New York Central doesn't buy too many of them, because they didn't. There were only two. Built by Alco-G.E. in 1926, they were numbered 1200-1201, and renumbered 300-301 in 1936. The units were converted to four diesel hump trailers in 1945. Ever alert to capture something unusual with his camera, Eddie photographed the 301 on October 16, 1938.

TOP: Before dieselization, heavy freight movements on the Electric Division were handled by class R-2 motors. Forty-two of these locomotives were built by Alco-G.E. in 1926 as NYC 1202-1243. They were renumbered to NYC 302-343 in 1936. The 313 is seen here on December 5, 1937.

ABOVE: Ed photographed the mother of all New York Central electric locomotives, S-1 motor 100, at Harmon on May 2, 1948. Built by Alco-G.E. in 1904 as NYC&HR 6000, she underwent extensive testing at Schenectady and was put into passenger service in 1906 along with 34 new S-2 motors. Originally built as 1-D-1 engines with single-axle pilot trucks at each end, all were converted to 2-D-2 engines following a tragic derailment in 1907. These were the locomotives that made an electrified Grand Central Terminal possible, and we are indeed fortunate that both G.C.T. and this pioneer locomotive have been preserved.

TOP: In 1908 and 1909, Twelve S-3 motors were added to the electric locomotive fleet, with a slightly lengthened wheelbase. Ed found the 145 in Harmon on December 5, 1937.

ABOVE: From 1913 through 1926, the Central's electric locomotive fleet was augmented by three classes of T motors: T-1, T-2, and T-3; the T-2's and T-3's each slightly larger and heavier than the earlier models. These were B-B+B-B locomotives, with all axles driven, and they were the standard for heavy passenger service into and out of Grand Central Terminal until the arrival of the rebuilt P motors that had originally been constructed for service in the Cleveland Union Terminal electrification. Motor 254 was a T-1b built by Alco-G.E. in 1913 and was photographed by Ed on his very fruitful visit to Harmon on December 5, 1937.

BELOW: With the Harmon roadway overpass in the background, T-2b 1168 waits for its next assignment on the 32.7-mile trip to Grand Central Terminal, which was actually in part uphill, although ever so slightly. The highest point between Grand Central and Albany was at the 125th Street Station in New York City, 43 feet above sea level. The 1168 is seen here on April 27, 1935, and it was renumbered 268 in 1936.

BOTTOM: The T-motors just kept getting bigger. The T-3's carbodies were about six and a half feet longer than those of the T-1 motors, but their end platforms were shorter, resulting in less than a foot difference in overall wheelbase. With an engineer's seat at both ends of these motors, end designation had to be redefined. On the T and P motors, the end with the overhead current collector was the front or number 1 end; the end with the steam heat boiler was the number 2 or rear end. T-3a 274 joined the electric fleet in November 1926. Bill Curtis photo taken on August 4, 1951.

BELOW: Twenty-two P-1a motors were built by Alco-G.E. for the Cleveland Union Terminal electrification project and delivered in 1929 and 1930, CUT 1050-1071, 200-221 in the 1936 renumbering. In 1951, almost three years before the CUT electrification was discontinued, motor 218 was rebuilt at Harmon to operate between Grand Central Terminal and Harmon. This was no minor undertaking; the CUT electrified territory functioned on 3,000 volts d.c. delivered by catenary, while the New York electrified territory used 660 volts d.c. supplied by under-running third rail. The pilot conversion engine was classed as P-2a and given road number 222. Roughly four years later, twenty more P-1a's moved east, were converted by General Electric to 660 volt operation, classed as P-2b's, and given road numbers 223-242. Here, in a Bill Curtis photo taken on July 14, 1951, is NYC 222, the first converted motor and the sole member of class P-2a.

OPPOSITE ABOVE: Sometimes, particularly in winter months, the steam boilers on Central's electric locomotives were not up to the task of heating a long train. To keep passengers warm and happy, the railroad invented the steam heat trailer, essentially an oil-fired steam boiler on wheels. I believe old steam locomotive tender frames were used for most, if not all, of the early models. H-7, seen here on April 4, 1936, was built in January 1932. Specifications state that its tanks carried 1,342 gallons of water and 204 gallons of oil, and that with an operating pressure of 155 pounds it could heat 16 cars for approximately 2.2 hours.

OPPOSITE BELOW: A later model steam heat trailer, H-20, came from the company shops at West Albany in 1947, having been rebuilt from an H5 tender. Ed caught it looking new and shiny at Harmon on April 13, 1947.

OPPOSITE ABOVE: Much of the local passenger traffic handled on Central's Electric Division, comprised mostly of workers who made daily treks between their bedroom communities north of the city and Gotham, was serviced by a huge fleet of multiple-unit cars. The roster of steel MU cars for 1943 lists 331 coaches, twelve passenger-baggage cars, four baggage-mail cars, and five baggage cars. Here, enjoying a day off outside the electric shop on October 16, 1938, is car 4251, one of twenty members of Lot 932. With 3-2 seating, 82 commuters could be packed into this car to enjoy their morning newspapers on the trip into the city, and their evening papers on the way home. Incidentally, folding an eight-column paper so that you could read it and not intrude on another passenger's space was a skill you quickly acquired. Heat for this car and most of the other MU coaches was by electricity, but a number of MU's were also equipped with steam heat so that they could be serviceable in winter behind steam power beyond the electrified trackage.

OPPOSITE BELOW: The MU coach fleet was augmented in 1950 by the arrival of 30 85-foot cars, NYC 4500-4529, in Lot 2207. Each car could seat 130 passengers in a 3-2 configuration. They were built by St. Louis Car Company and were further augmented by an additional 70 cars, 4530-4599, in the same lot. Ed photographed brand-new 4502 on May 21, 1950.

ABOVE: Budd's first order for its revolutionary Rail Diesel Cars (RDC's) was placed by, you guessed it, New York Central, which purchased in 1950 two RDC-1's, M450 and M451, for use on subsidiary Boston and Albany. By August of 1951, two RDC-1's, M454 and M455, were making regular runs between Harmon and Peekskill on the Hudson Division. M455 sits bright and new at Harmon in a Bill Curtis photo taken on August 25, 1951.

BELOW: Before leaving Harmon, we'll pause to watch J1e Hudson 5327 departing west with #157, a Poughkeepsie local. To say that this little four-car train is being handled with ease by this thoroughbred locomotive would be an understatement. It's June 18, 1938. I hope you have enjoyed this nostalgic visit to one of the most interesting locations on the New York Central System. I also hope you'll join Ed and me as we follow the path of #157 up the Hudson River to Poughkeepsie and then on to Albany in Volume 2 of *New York Central Power Along the Hudson*.

BIBLIOGRAPHY

Edson, William D., and Vail, H. L., Jr. *Steam Locomotives of the New York Central Lines, Part 1.* Cleveland, Ohio: New York Central System Historical Society, Inc., 1997.

Harmon, the New City on the Hudson (Real Estate Brochure). 1908.

Haas, Arnold, *Memories of New York Central Steam*, River Vale, New Jersey: D. Carleton Railbooks, 1980.

History of the Town of Cortlandt. Croton, New York: Town of Cortlandt Bicentennial History Committee, 1988.

Lederer, Richard M, Jr. *The Place Names of Westchester County.* Harrison, New York: Harbor Hill Books, 1978.

May, Edward L. and Edson, William D. *Locomotives of the New York Central Lines.* Irvington-on-Hudson, New York: Edson-May Publications, 1966.

New York Central System Historical Society, *Headlight* Vol. V, No. 2 (May 1975); Vol. V, No. 4 (November 1975); Vol. VI, No. 2 (May 1976); and Vol. VI, No. 4 (November 1976).

Staufer, Alvin F. *Steam Power of the New York Central System, Vol. 1.* Leroy, Ohio: Alvin F. Staufer, 1961.

Staufer, Alvin F. *New York Central's Early Power.* Carrolton, Ohio: Alvin F. Staufer, 1967.

Staufer, Alvin F. *Thoroughbreds.* Medina, Ohio: Alvin F. Staufer, 1974.

Staufer, Alvin F. and May, Edward L. *New York Central's Later Power 1910-1968.* Medina, Ohio: Alvin F. Staufer, 1981.

Also various Hudson Division/Mohawk Division employee timetables, public timetables, locomotive classification books, and rule books, published by the New York Central Railroad; as well as various editions of *The Official Guide of the Railways*, published by the National Railway Publication Company. All from the author's collection.